T0282860

In 1994, when I was about five years into my recovery, my sponsor gave me Stephanie Covington's *A Woman's Way through the Twelve Steps*. I can only imagine how many millions of women have finally been able to connect to their recovery through this classic—and now transgender and nonbinary individuals will be able to see themselves in recovery literature, too. Ever the visionary, Dr. Covington has yet again made women's recovery more accessible and inclusive. The workbook and facilitator guide are the tools needed to ensure that many millions more women benefit from this brilliant and accessible work.

Dawn Nickel
Cofounder, SHE RECOVERS® Foundation
Author of *She Recovers Every Day*

———

As CEO of an agency that includes six gender-specific women's treatment programs, I have had the benefit of hearing from numerous counselors and clinicians who have used *A Woman's Way through the Twelve Steps* workbook and facilitator guide. All have shared my view that they are a wonderful resource that provides a reflective and empowering approach to recovery, uniquely designed for women. The workbook's exercises offer priceless support for those who seek healing and change, while the facilitator guide offers professionals in the field valuable direction. I have also seen the empowering effect these materials can have on recovery and personal growth.

Jeanne McAlister
Founder and CEO, McAlister Institute of Treatment and Education

———

A Woman's Way through the Twelve Steps was a groundbreaking work that reflected Dr. Stephanie Covington's tireless advocacy to ensure that the needs of women in recovery were fully met. In the 30th anniversary edition, Dr. Covington has done a great deal of work to update the language and truly make the shift from gender-specific care to gender-responsive care. This workbook serves as a lovely companion to the updated book and will help all women on a Twelve Step path of recovery engage in the Steps more fully and meaningfully.

Dr. Jamie Marich
Author of *Trauma and the 12 Steps* and *Dissociation Made Simple*
Founder and Director, The Institute for Creative Mindfulness

———

Written in 1939, the original Twelve Steps of AA have helped millions of people around the world. But as they were developed by men for men and reflected the knowledge of addiction at that time, the voices of women and gender-expansive people were not included or even conceived of.

Stephanie Covington changed that with her seminal publication of *A Woman's Way through the Twelve Steps,* published in 1994. For the first time, the voices of women in recovery were illuminated.

In the updated version of that work, Dr. Covington includes new information on the impact of trauma as well as the voices of many more women and gender-expansive people sharing their challenges, triumphs, experience, strength, and hope.

With a trauma-informed and gender-expansive lens, Dr. Covington allows so many more people to be "seen" and "heard" while sharing the powerful healing experience of inclusivity.

The facilitator guide and the participant workbook complete the package. Women can personalize their recovery journey and have something to refer to for years to come. The facilitator guide allows professionals and nonprofessionals alike to run groups with confidence.

As a trainer, consultant, and colleague of Dr. Covington's and a retired director of treatment centers for co-occurring disorders, I have witnessed over and over the transformational power of her work.

Thank you, Dr. Covington, for listening and including our voices.

Carol Ackley, LADC
CEO, retired, RiverRidge Treatment Centers

Dr. Stephanie Covington has developed a companion workbook to her book *A Woman's Way through the Twelve Steps. A Woman's Way through the Twelve Steps Workbook* is so useful and beneficial to women on their recovery journey. Dr. Covington has an inviting way for women to begin to think differently about the Twelve Steps and how they can help in women's desire for recovery. The focus is on spirituality, not religion. Dr. Covington thoughtfully formatted the workbook to include self-soothing exercises for awareness, and she ends each Step with gratitude for learning and growth. Asking women to journal their responses has a profound effect on each person and allows for additional processing for long-term healing. *A Woman's Way through the Twelve Steps Workbook* is essential for women working through the Twelve Steps!

Sandy Clark, MS, LPCC, LADC, NCACII, SAP Therapist, Educator
President of Minnesota Addiction Professionals
Author of *Charlie the Therapy Dog*

Women and gender-diverse people in recovery can use this workbook that Dr. Covington has developed to explore their inner world on an as-ready basis, deepening their experience of the Twelve Steps and working through trauma residue, if present. The workbook is not a substitute for professional help if it is needed, but with the help of an astute sponsor, recovering women can use it to develop an understanding of what makes them tick and what experiences contributed to their addictive behaviors. The workbook provides an important experience for women in recovery who are ready to dig deeper into their history, allowing them to identify potential triggers for relapse and unresolved grief for losses prior to and resulting from their addiction. It is a comprehensive template for exploring the many causes and aspects of addiction, providing recovering women and their sponsors an outline that can be returned to many times.

Lorie Dwinell, LCSW
Retired Clinical Social Worker
Coauthor of *After the Tears: Helping Adult Children of
Alcoholics Heal Their Childhood Trauma*

Progressing through the lessons, participants reflect on personal journeys and, through myriad activities, identify context around harmful and helpful decisions and choices. Numerous activities and exercises can be done regardless of place, economics, and personal challenges. They allow participants to "try on" certain perspectives to see if they fit, to recognize how these perspectives may have contributed to harmful activity, and to identify strengths and develop stepping stones for moving forward.

Maureen Buell,
Retired, National Institute of Corrections

UPDATED AND EXPANDED EDITION

A
WOMAN'S
WAY
THROUGH THE
TWELVE STEPS

WORKBOOK

Stephanie S. Covington, PhD, LCSW

Hazelden Publishing

Hazelden Publishing
Center City, Minnesota 55012
hazelden.org/bookstore

©2000, 2024 by Stephanie S. Covington
All rights reserved. First edition published 2000.
Updated and expanded edition published 2024.
Printed in the United States of America

No part of this publication, either print or electronic, may be reproduced in any form or by any means without the express written permission of the publisher. Failure to comply with these terms may expose you to legal action and damages for copyright infringement.

ISBN: 978-1-63634-073-9

Editor's Notes

The Spiral of Addiction and Recovery illustration on page 2 and the Self-Soothing Chart on page 98 are adapted from *Helping Women Recover*. Copyright 1999, revised 2008 and 2019 by S. Covington. This material is used by permission of John Wiley & Sons, Inc.

Some names, details, and circumstances have been changed to protect the privacy of those mentioned in this publication.

This publication is not intended as a substitute for the advice of health care professionals. Readers should be aware that websites listed in this work may have changed or disappeared between when this work was written and when it is read.

The Twelve Steps are reprinted from *Alcoholics Anonymous,* 4th ed. (New York: Alcoholics Anonymous World Services, 2001), 59–60. Alcoholics Anonymous, AA, and the Big Book are registered trademarks of Alcoholics Anonymous World Services, Inc. Hazelden Publishing offers a variety of information on addiction and other areas. The views and interpretations herein are those of the author and are neither endorsed nor approved by AA or any Twelve Step organization.

Cover design: Sara Streifel, Think Creative Design
Interior design and typesetting: Sara Streifel, Think Creative Design
Developmental editor: Susan Rose
Production editor: April Ebb

AUTHOR'S NOTE ABOUT THE COVER DESIGN

I see the lotus as a symbol of women's recovery, so I again chose the lotus for the new cover of this updated and expanded edition of *A Woman's Way through the Twelve Steps Workbook*. A lotus is a powerful symbol of resilience and transformation, two aspects of women's recovery. Lotuses rise from muddy waters to blossom. Although they grow with their roots deep in the mud, they emerge pure and unblemished. They unfold gradually, one petal at a time, to blossom in the sunlight.

The mud symbolizes murky beginnings, the material world, or the darkness of addiction. The water symbolizes experience, transition, or recovery. The lotus symbolizes the purity of the soul, rebirth, spiritual awakening, transformation, and enlightenment. For thousands of years, and in many religious traditions, the lotus has been associated with spiritual practices and a detachment from illusions.

Recovery is a transformational experience, a fundamental change. When a woman recovers, she is able to say, "Who I am today is not who I was." The elegant and beautiful lotus flower that emerges from the mud is the beautiful woman within.

CONTENTS

CONTENTS

Beginning *A Woman's Way through the Twelve Steps*

Since 1935, when Alcoholics Anonymous (AA) was founded, more and more women and people of diverse gender experience have entered recovery programs based on the Twelve Steps of AA. The AA program was developed with heterosexual men as the presumed audience and was not designed to include or address the experiences of women and LGBTQ+ people. But women and LGBTQ+ people have their own needs in recovery. Even more, we are learning that each person's recovery is unique, and there is no one right way to proceed in "working" the Steps. This workbook is designed to help you create your own path of recovery.

Using the Steps as guides, you will explore what you think, feel, and believe. Then you will connect this inner life to your actions with other people in the world around you. This experience of connecting your feelings and beliefs (your inner life) with your actions (your outer life) is what I call *wholeness* or *integrity*.

The Steps provide principles for living. These principles can help you develop integrity. The aim of the Steps is for your life to be congruent with your deepest values. The Steps will help you discover what your values are; then they will help you see how you may have acted contrary to your values in the past and how you can act in harmony with them in the future.

You will come back to this theme of aligning your inner and outer lives throughout your journey. Progressing in recovery is like climbing a spiral staircase: you cycle up and away from a life that revolved around addiction. Instead of continuing a downward spiral into ever-tighter circles around the addiction, in recovery you spiral upward into ever-widening circles of self-knowledge, freedom, and connection to others. In addiction your inner and outer lives are constricted; in recovery your life expands. The diagram on the next page illustrates this.

The Spiral of Addiction and Recovery

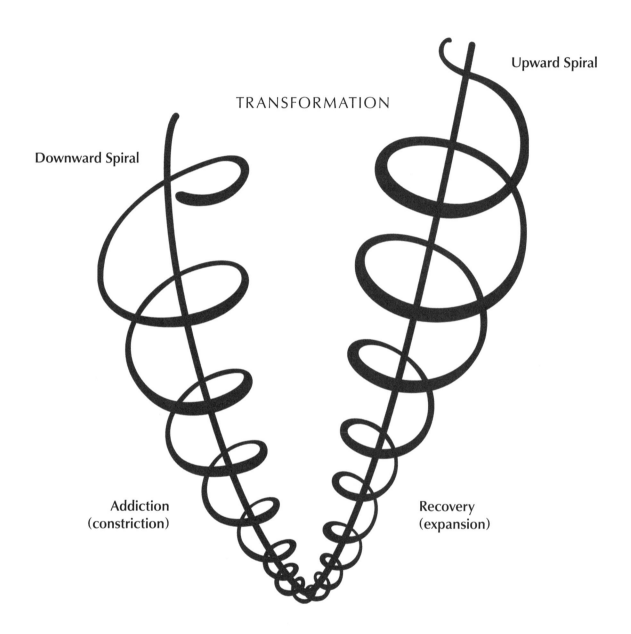

TRANSFORMATION

Downward Spiral

Upward Spiral

Addiction
(constriction)

Recovery
(expansion)

Adapted from *Helping Women Recover*. Copyright 1999, revised 2008 and 2019 by S. Covington. This material is used by permission of John Wiley & Sons, Inc.

We recover in connection with others, not in isolation. That is why the Twelve Steps speak of "we" rather than "I." As you work through this workbook, feel free to discuss your experiences of the exercises with others whom you are connected to on the journey of recovery, especially your sponsor.

This workbook is a companion to the book *A Woman's Way through the Twelve Steps*. You will benefit from reading about each Step in the book before covering that Step in this workbook. Many recovering women were interviewed for *A Woman's Way*, and you will see some of their words quoted throughout this workbook. They are cited not as "experts," but rather as companions on the journey who are sharing their experience, strength, and hope. Occasionally, additional quotations from *A Woman's Way* are used to help illustrate the points in this workbook.

Each Step, or chapter, includes exercises to help you explore your inner and outer lives. At the end of each Step, you are invited to practice an exercise for "self-soothing." In the past most of us used addictive substances or compulsive behaviors to soothe ourselves. In recovery we need to find new sources of comfort. Because alcohol and other drugs tend to numb our feelings, in early recovery we often find ourselves flooded with unfamiliar emotions. These emotions can feel overwhelming, so we need to find ways to handle or soothe these emotions—ways that don't involve addictive behaviors.

Self-Soothing: The Five Senses

One way to soothe yourself is by doing the Five Senses exercise. Here is a picture of the exercise.

Whenever you feel anxious, it is helpful to look around the place you are in and go through these five steps, focusing on each sense and naming what you can identify. This exercise can help you stay in the present. Often when we are anxious or fearful it is because we are thinking about or feeling something from the past or worrying about the future.

5 things

4 things

3 things

2 things

1 thing

Reprinted from *Healing Trauma+: A Brief Intervention for Women and Gender-Diverse People* by Stephanie S. Covington and Eileen M. Russo (Center City, MN: Hazelden, 2021).

The Group Agreements

To make these sessions as safe and helpful as possible, our group will adhere to these group agreements.

1. **Attendance.** Your commitment to attend each session is important, not only for your own benefit in understanding the Twelve Steps but also because it is necessary to create an environment of mutual support. If you must miss a session, please let me know beforehand.

2. **Confidentiality.** Nothing that anyone else says in this room is to be repeated outside that session. We need to know that we can trust one another, and there can be no trust if people are concerned that information about them may be shared with others or if group members gossip about one another. The exception is that I am required by law to reveal if a member's personal safety or the safety of another person is at stake.

3. **Safety.** For everyone to feel safe in this group, we all need to agree that there will be no verbal or physical abuse in our sessions.

4. **Participation.** Every person's participation is important. It is not helpful if some people dominate our discussions and others remain silent. Please let other people finish what they're saying before you add your comments. If you would rather not talk about a particular subject, you have the option to pass. When you have something to say, please share your remarks with the whole group and refrain from having side conversations.

5. **Honesty.** Nobody will pressure you to tell anything about yourself that you don't want to talk about, but when you do talk, tell the truth about what's happened to you and how you feel. Also, please talk about your personal experiences, rather than about people in general.

6. **Respect.** Showing mutual respect is important to the group. That means nobody criticizes, judges, or talks down to anyone. If you think that someone is showing disrespect to someone else, please say so respectfully. Even if you feel uncomfortable at some point and don't want to participate, show your respect by not disrupting the group. You can be quiet until you feel more comfortable and are ready to participate again.

7. **Questions.** If you have a question about anything, please ask. Please also show respect for other people's questions.

8. **Focus.** Try to stick to the topic the group is exploring. If you think that we're getting off the topic, feel free to mention that.

9. **Punctuality.** We'll start on time and end on time. The times of our group meetings are

_____.

Additional agreements if your group has added them:

First Thing in the Morning

1. What are five things you do automatically upon waking? List them in order.

1. _____

2. _____

3. _____

4. _____

5. _____

2. What does it feel like when you do things differently?

Balancing the Scale

3. In the left column, list the parts of your life that support your addictive behaviors. In the right column, list the areas that encourage and support you in your recovery.

Support for my addiction	Support for my recovery

4. How can you increase the support for your recovery?

Each Step in this workbook ends with an invitation to think about what you are grateful for. In early recovery it's sometimes hard to recognize and name these things. However, as women in recovery, we often find we learn a great deal every day and have many reasons for gratitude. Thankfulness is a skill that strengthens us, and you will have a chance to practice it.

I hope this workbook becomes a personal record of your recovery, one that you will treasure years from now when you look back on this part of your journey through the Twelve Steps.

STEP ONE

*We admitted we were powerless over alcohol—
that our lives had become unmanageable.*

Step One is about *awareness* and *unmanageability*. Before admitting something, we first need to be aware of it. We need to become conscious of our feelings, our behavior, and their effects on other people and ourselves. The opposite of awareness is denial. When we deny something exists, we can't change it. Only when we tell ourselves the truth—risk seeing ourselves as we are—can we begin to make changes.

When we begin to break through our denial, we will become aware that we've lost the ability to manage our lives. We have lost the ability to choose consistently whether or how much we will drink, use another drug, binge on food, pursue destructive sexual relationships, gamble, or do whatever behavior has sent our lives spiraling out of control. Maybe we've lost a job, a spouse, children, money, or friends because of this addictive behavior. Or our lives may look intact on the outside: we're still going to work, taking care of our children, and keeping up our appearance. But inside and hidden, our emotions are in disarray and our lives are a house of cards that could tumble at any time.

In this first chapter you will begin to increase your awareness about your life and especially about the addiction you are focusing on. You will also examine your life to see whether you can honestly say, "I am managing my life well."

Since this workbook can be used to explore a variety of addictive behaviors, it will be helpful for you to identify clearly which addiction you are exploring. It might be your drinking, other drug use, eating habits, gambling, spending, sexual relationships, or something else.

If you are concerned about several behaviors, choose one to focus on. Afterward, if you like, you can go through the workbook again, examining a different addiction.

The addiction I am exploring in this workbook is my _____.

Awareness

1. Think back over the past few weeks. How have you obsessed or fantasized about your addictive behavior? Name three times you have done this. Try to be as specific as possible.

   EXAMPLE:

   Yesterday afternoon at work, I zoned out for more than half an hour thinking about . . .

2. Think about the six months immediately before you became abstinent (or the past six months if you are not yet abstinent). Give at least one example of a time when you:

   • lied about, hid, or minimized your addiction

   • did something that harmed others because of your addiction

• felt guilty or ashamed about your behavior

• tried to relieve pain caused by your addictive behavior

• tried to get others to support your addiction

One of the main truths we need to become aware of is that we have power in some areas of our lives but are powerless over other things. In *A Woman's Way through the Twelve Steps*, Maria observes:

> Women have always been powerless. So admitting I'm powerless over alcohol is really a way to keep the power I do have. I'm admitting that there's something I can't control and that by trying to control it, I am going to lose even more power than I'd already lost by virtue of my being female.
>
> — MARIA —

Oddly enough, acknowledging our lack of power over things we can't control frees us to act in areas where we do have some power.

3.   Below, make two lists. On the left, list things in your life you can't control (areas where you don't have power). On the right, list issues in your life that you do have some control over (areas where you may have some power).

Things I *can't* control/have no power over	Things I *can* control/have some power over
EXAMPLE: *getting older*	**EXAMPLE:** *the way I treat myself and other women who are getting older*

In which of the lists did you put the following?

• your addictive behavior

• other people's behaviors

• the decision to seek recovery

• the decision to ask for and accept help

• the care you give to yourself

• the support you give to others in recovery

Unmanageability

4. Vivian heard someone in a meeting ask, "If you hired someone like you to manage your life, would you continue paying her?"

   How would you answer that question? Include what you like and what you don't like in your answer.

   EXAMPLE:

   The woman managing my life can't seem to finish tasks. She thinks about food when she needs to be getting something done. Then she feels bad about not accomplishing anything, but instead of getting back to work, she eats until she's numb.

5. Read the following list of signs that life has become unmanageable. Next, check the ones that apply to you and fill in the spaces at the end of the sentences as appropriate for you. Finally, list as many other signs of unmanageability in your life as you can think of. You may want to use the ones you put on your downward spiral.

   ☐ I micromanage my life to avoid feeling empty, anxious, or worthless.

   ☐ I start the day committed to not drink, but by midday, I've lost track of how much I've had to drink.

   ☐ I've embarrassed myself in public.

   ☐ I've lost my relationship with _____.

   ☐ I've lost _____.

☐ My feelings are in an uproar much of the time.

☐ I'm numb most of the time.

☐ I live in fear that my carefully constructed world will fall apart.

☐ _____

☐ _____

☐ _____

☐ _____

☐ _____

☐ _____

> Breaking my value system in my addiction played on my shame.
> I'd tell myself, "I'll never drive drunk when I pick up the kids after
> school," and then I would. That triggered my core sense of being
> unworthy, and then I wanted to move out of relationship. I wanted to
> hide and break the very connections that meant the most to me.
>
> — DARLENE —

6. If you feel ready to do so, complete the following statement, sign it, and date it.

I admit I am powerless over _____. My life is unmanageable.

_____   _____
SIGNATURE   DATE

Self-Soothing: Listen for a New Voice

Congratulations! You have made a significant beginning on your journey of recovery. Take a break to do something good for yourself. Think about what you will do to relax or celebrate now that you're not using your addictive behavior to soothe yourself. Here are some possibilities:

Listen for a New Voice

Admitting you are powerless does not mean admitting you are worthless. Nothing could be further from the truth! If acknowledging that your addiction is a problem causes you to feel your inner self is bad or hateful, try this exercise. Read the paragraphs below, then close your eyes and repeat the affirmations aloud. If you have a friend who can read the paragraphs aloud to you while your eyes are shut, that would be even better.

> Imagine that you are in a small room. The windows are shut. The door is locked. In this room you hear all the negative voices that plague you. Perhaps they tell you that you're selfish for wanting something better than the life you now have. Maybe they say that you're worthless because of the things you've done in your life so far.

> Now imagine that acknowledging your powerlessness over your addiction has unlocked the door. You open the door. Outside is an open meadow bathed in sunlight. As you walk through the door, you're aware that the negative voices stay behind you in the room. Step outside, into the sunlight.

> Now that you're outside, you become aware of a new voice, a quiet voice. This voice says, "You deserve to be taken seriously. You deserve to be accepted without judgment. You deserve to ask for and receive help. Help is here."

> Now keep your eyes closed and repeat these affirmations out loud:
>
> » I deserve to be taken seriously.
>
> » I deserve to be accepted without judgment.
>
> » I deserve to ask for and receive help.

It's important to say these affirmations *out loud* so that you hear them spoken with your own voice.

Other Self-Soothing Possibilities

- Go for a walk somewhere beautiful, such as a park, a nature area, a zoo, botanical gardens, or anywhere with landscaping.

- Pet a furry animal.

- Watch some birds.

- Swim or take a bath and enjoy the feeling of water on your body.

- Ask for a hug.

- Call a friend.

- Lie down, close your eyes, and do nothing.

- Watch rain or a sunset or the clouds floating by.

- Listen to music that lifts your spirits, and maybe move your body to the music.

- _____

- _____

- _____

Gratitude

Chances are, if you're starting recovery, you've had some bleak moments lately. It's important to gain encouragement from the bright spots in your day. It's important to cultivate gratitude. Write down one thing you've gained from working on Step One that you're grateful for.

EXAMPLES:

I've been sober for two weeks.

I don't feel the pressure to pretend anymore.

I'm learning to tell the difference between what I can control and what I can't.

STEP TWO

Came to believe that a Power greater than ourselves could restore us to sanity.

The key ideas in Step Two are *faith* and *sanity.* Faith includes the ideas of belief and trust. Many of us enter recovery thinking that nothing and no one can be trusted. We may be skeptical about belief in a Higher Power. We often feel confused about what we believe. We may have learned from bitter experience that many people cannot be trusted.

Trusting someone can feel risky, yet Step Two asserts that in order to recover, we need to find someone or something we can trust. Step Two asks us to entertain the possibility that *help is available,* that we cannot and need not rely only on our selves to break from our addiction. We are not told who or what this Power is. Instead, we are invited to explore for ourselves and make up our own minds. *Coming to believe* means setting aside our illusion of control and opening ourselves to the possibility of support.

This Step also asks us to admit that we have done some out-of-control and regrettable things in our unmanageable lives. Some may find needed support through a mental health diagnosis, but that is not the "insanity" implied in this Step. Maybe we grew up in "crazy-making" families and came to doubt our perceptions of reality. Maybe we did irrational things—harmful to ourselves or others—because of our addiction. The traditional AA definition of *insanity* is "doing the same thing over and over, expecting different results." Step Two invites us to step onto a different path; by living differently, we can expect different results.

In this chapter, you will explore the idea of belief—what does it mean to believe something? You will also have a chance to think about what you believe. Then you will look back at your life to identify things you may have done that felt "insane," as well as forward into the future to envision the sanity you want.

Faith

We all believe in something, even though sometimes we take those beliefs for granted.

1. List five things you have faith in—five things you trust.

    EXAMPLES:

    I trust that the sun will rise tomorrow, and I will continue to believe this even if the sun is hidden behind clouds.

    I trust that if I drop a rock, it will fall, not rise.

    1. _____

    2. _____

    3. _____

    4. _____

    5. _____

2. The most important thing we need to believe or trust in recovery is that *help is available.* We are not entirely on our own. What evidence, if any, do you have that might lead you to believe that help is available to you in recovery? Try to state at least three pieces of evidence, no matter how tiny they seem.

    EXAMPLE:

    This workbook and its companion book are here to help me recover.

3. Beliefs have a huge effect on how we feel and what we do. Below are two opposing beliefs. Take a few minutes to imagine yourself having the first belief. Write down how you would *feel* and what you would *do* if you believed in your gut that Belief A were true. Then do the same for Belief B.

BELIEF A:

Good things do happen, but the universe is essentially a cold, hostile place in which I can trust only myself.

• How would you *feel* if you were convinced of Belief A?

• How would you *live this week* if you thought Belief A were true?

BELIEF B:

Bad things do happen, but the universe is essentially a safe place in which someone or something has my best interests at heart.

• How would you *feel* if you were confident of Belief B?

• How would you *live this week* if you thought Belief B were true?

4. Step Two asks you to entertain the possibility that Belief B might be true. Put another way, it asks you to *act as if* Belief B is true and notice what happens. What do you think right now regarding this belief? Check any of the following responses that apply to you, or describe your thoughts.

    ☐ I am completely and wholeheartedly convinced of Belief B.

    ☐ I believe Belief B partly, but I also have doubts.

    ☐ I don't believe it, but I'm open to evidence that might help me come to believe it.

    ☐ I don't believe it, but I'm willing to act as if Belief B is true for a while and see what happens.

    ☐ I don't believe it, and I'm not open to it either.

    ☐ Other: _____

5. Set aside the expectations held by your community, your family, or anyone in your love life. How do *you* currently feel about the idea of a Power greater than yourself? (You can check more than one feeling if you're feeling several things at once.)

    ☐ comforted   ☐ threatened   ☐ scared   ☐ angry

    ☐ hopeful   ☐ excited   ☐ confused   ☐ skeptical

    ☐ awed   ☐ other: _____

Step Two does not require us to think of our Higher Power in any particular way. Some of us have embraced a masculine God as the first male figure we could really trust. Others feel more comfortable with feminine, neutral, or personal images of a Higher Power. A Mother Goddess, an Inner Light, a Life Force, a Creative Intelligence—these are all possible ways of thinking about our Higher Power. In fact, we don't have to imagine the Power as "higher" at all. Perhaps we believe in an Inner Power that is greater than the self we project to the people around us. We might even look to the healing spirit embodied in our recovery group. The strength in our group could be the Power greater than ourselves. Step Two leaves us entirely free to make up our own minds about the Power we are going to trust, as long as we choose a Power that is supportive of our recovery.

6. What do you currently believe about a Power greater than yourself?

    EXAMPLES:

    I am a Muslim and I believe in Allah, who is . . .

    I don't believe in any god or goddess, but I have experienced a Power greater than myself in my recovery group.

    I don't know what I believe about a Higher Power.

God is not an abstract God or a higher-up God that I find
alone. To experience God, I have to have other people in my
life. . . . It really is *our* power—it's not mine, or yours, not
theirs, but *ours*. It's only power because it's shared.

— RUTH —

The Power of Support

7. List some ways you would like to feel supported by your community. You can include examples of both emotional and practical support.

_____

_____

_____

_____

8. How would you feel if your community supported you in these ways?

Sanity

9. When you were deep in your addiction, did you ever do things that felt "insane" to you or others? If so, what were some of the things you did? If you created a collage during the group session, what did you have on it?

    EXAMPLES:

    I vowed to quit drinking and poured out all the alcohol in the house, but went out and bought more the very next day.

    I treated my drugs as more important than my children.

10. When you think of yourself as "restored to sanity," what picture of yourself comes to mind? If you did a collage in group, what did you have on it?

11. In the space below, describe or draw yourself as "sane." You may want to write a poem or draw with colored pencils, pastels, ink, or crayons. Use words or images to express the sanity you're heading toward. Look at this image or read this description when you need some extra encouragement.

OPTIONAL PROJECT

Ask two people in your recovery group to tell you about their Higher Power and how their Higher Power has helped them gain sanity. Record here what you learn.

12. Someone might read Step Two as saying we should wait passively for something outside ourselves to restore us to sanity. In reality, we need to actively choose to be recovering people who are open to a Higher Power. What is one thing you can do today to choose sanity?

I'm an engineer, a scientist. I tried experiments in staying sober by myself for two years. I tried over and over again, and found that if I try to stay sober by myself, it doesn't work no matter what.

— SHERIE —

Self-Soothing: Contemplating Nature

Contemplating something beautiful and predictable in nature can help us believe there's something in the world we can trust. Choose something from nature that you can focus on for a while. If you live near the beach, you could sit and listen to the waves for half an hour. If you have a park nearby, you could watch the leaves on a tree rustle in the breeze. You could lie on the grass and watch the clouds. You could watch the moon rise or the sun set. Let the beauty of this thing that happens day after day soak into your bones.

Gratitude

Write down one thing you've gained from working on Step Two that you're grateful for.

EXAMPLES:

I'm realizing that I'm not alone in my experience of feeling crazy.

I'm letting people in my recovery group get to know me.

STEP THREE

*Made a decision to turn our will and our lives over to
the care of God as we understood Him.*

Step Three deals with three issues: *control, surrender,* and *decision-making.* In Step One, we
learned that there are many things in life we can't control. In Step Two, we entertained the possibility that we might not have to control everything, because there is something or someone
good in the universe we can trust. In Step Three, we decide to act on that possibility. We decide
to let this spiritual power guide our lives rather than trying to control life ourselves.

Giving up control (or letting go) of the things we can't and don't have to control involves
learning several skills. The first is the skill of wisdom: recognizing the difference between things
we can change and things we can't. The second is the skill of surrender. Surrender is different
from submission to a force that wants to control us. Many of us know how to either control or
be controlled by someone, but surrendering—opening ourselves to the guidance of a mentor
without falling under someone's control—may be a new experience. The third skill deals with
making wise decisions. Many of us feel relatively comfortable making decisions in our roles
at work or with our families, but we lack confidence in making decisions to care for our inner
selves. Others are unaccustomed to being decisive in any area of our lives.

In this chapter, you will learn about control and practice the skills of wisdom, surrender, and
decision-making. You may have spent many years building your control muscles; now you will
start building your "turning it over" muscles.

Control

As much as we might want to control what other people and the rest of the world do, we can't. The truth is, we can be responsible *only for ourselves*—our own actions and attitudes. Everything else is beyond our control. In Twelve Step meetings we hear the Serenity Prayer:

God, grant me the serenity

to accept the things I cannot change,

courage to change the things I can,

and wisdom to know the difference.

1.   Look back at your lists in question 3 of Step One (page 10). There you listed some things you can control and some things you can't. Using the Serenity Prayer as your guide, check your lists. Would you move anything from one column to the other? Can you think of anything you might add?

Try to add three more things that you can't control and three more things you can. Remember: you *can* control your own actions and attitudes.

Things I *can't* control/have no power over	Things I *can* control/have some power over

> I think probably 90 percent of life is beyond our control—the weather, other people, happenstance. I worry that things will happen to my daughter, but there's only so much I can do. I can lock the household poisons in a cabinet, but I can't control a drunk driver who runs a red light. Worrying about uncontrollable things just robs us of the time we have.
>
> — JULIA —

Surrender

Surrendering our will and our lives to our Higher Power is very different from waiting to be rescued by a male authority who will take care of us as long as we behave. Surrender is simply letting go of our need to control, releasing ourselves into the stream of life, and trusting we will be held afloat.

2. Here's an exercise to help you think about surrender:

    Think of a problem or challenge you are currently facing. Make a fist with one hand, and imagine yourself gripping that problem tightly. Grip as hard as you can. Feel the muscles in your arm tighten. They might hurt or feel tired. Your shoulders and neck might feel tight as well. Feel what it's like to grip that problem.

    Now let go: Slowly open your hand. Let your fingers uncurl. Feel your muscles relaxing. This is what surrender feels like.

    Describe this experience. Write a couple of sentences about what it felt like to let go.

3. To remember the difference between surrender and either submission or control, it might help to draw some pictures.

> First, draw a picture of yourself controlling something. For example, you might draw yourself huddled over a precious box, protecting it from being stolen.

> Next, draw yourself submitting to someone else's control. You might draw yourself with your head bowed, while someone takes your precious box away.

> Finally, draw yourself surrendering. You could draw yourself sitting at a short distance from your box, with your head up and your hands open, relaxed.

4. We often need to surrender one day or one hour at a time. What are two things that help you surrender?

   EXAMPLES:

   going to a meeting, carrying a worry stone in my pocket

   reciting the Serenity Prayer, calling my sponsor

   _____

   _____

Decision-Making

5. Many of us have not learned how to make wise decisions yet. Here is a process you can use for any decision:

   a. Choose an area of your life you want to consider turning over to the care of your Higher Power. This area might be a relationship, the way you use money, a situation at work, the way you care for your body—anything. Write down what this area of your life is.

      EXAMPLE:

      my relationship with my boyfriend

      _____

b. Focus on how you have been behaving in this area of your life. Remember that you can make decisions only about what you will do. As you look at yourself in this situation, what do you observe about your behavior?

EXAMPLE:

I continue to live with him while he gets drunk and I'm in recovery. I don't say anything when he spends our shared money on alcohol. I rarely voice disagreements with him. When he urges me to have a drink, I just leave the room.

c. What have *others told you* about your behavior in this situation? Has your sponsor said anything about it?

EXAMPLE:

My sponsor says I am being too passive. I'm endangering my own recovery and enabling my boyfriend to stay in his addiction.

d. How do you *feel* about this situation? How do you feel about your behavior?

EXAMPLE:

I feel ashamed for not standing up to him more than I do. I feel afraid to challenge him because I'm afraid he'll leave me. I'm afraid I can't survive on my own. I feel ashamed for being afraid of this. I'm proud of myself that I've chosen to be in recovery even though he laughs at me.

e. What *conclusions* can you draw from these observations and feelings? What can you learn about yourself? About the situation? (In other words, what do your feelings and your behavior show you?)

EXAMPLE:

I think my fear of living on my own is leading to choices that aren't good for my recovery. They're not good for my boyfriend either.

f. Review your answers to questions (b) through (e). What *action* will you decide to take in light of these conclusions?

EXAMPLE:

I need to tell my boyfriend that I can't live with someone who gets drunk every day. Nor will I help him buy alcohol because it's bad for my recovery and bad for him. It's scary for me to think about telling him this. I'm going to talk to my sponsor about this and see what she thinks. Maybe I need to make plans to have somewhere else to go for a while before I talk to my boyfriend.

In Step Three, I release who I thought I was and let go of that image so something else can come in. The moment of surrender is when I allow for the possibility that I can act differently, even though I don't know what I'm supposed to do.

— MARTA —

Self-Soothing: Breathing Meditation

Meditation is a valuable tool for learning to surrender—to let go. You will learn more about meditation in Step Eleven, but you can experiment with one form of meditation now. It deals simply with breathing. Read through these instructions, then try them out.

> Sit in a quiet place, free from distractions. Sit up straight and place your feet flat on the floor. (If you prefer, you may sit on the floor.)
>
> Empty your hands and lap so that you are not holding anything. Close your eyes and pay attention to the breath at the tip of your nose. (If you prefer, you may focus your eyes on a single object, such as a candle flame.)
>
> Slowly count to four as you breathe in. Then count to four as you breathe out. Try to keep doing this for about five minutes. If a thought comes into your mind, just acknowledge it and let it go. Then go back to focusing on your breathing. (You might want to set a timer so that you won't be distracted thinking about the time.)
>
> Don't be too concerned about the thoughts that tumble into your mind when you try to focus. Don't get frustrated with yourself for not doing the exercise "right." Just observe the thoughts and let them go.

Gratitude

Write down one thing you've gained from working on Step Three that you're grateful for.

EXAMPLES:

I'm getting better at recognizing things I can't control.

I made a decision I feel good about.

STEP FOUR

*Made a searching and fearless moral
inventory of ourselves.*

Two important questions are raised in Step Four: What does it mean to be *fearless* and what does it mean to take an *inventory* of ourselves? Fear is exactly the reaction many people have to the idea of taking a self-inventory. A "moral inventory" brings up images of judgment, of being tried and found guilty.

It's more helpful to see a self-inventory as the kind of thorough housecleaning most homes need from time to time. It's a chance to sort through things, deciding what to keep and what to toss. It's a self-exploration, a chance to discover "Who am I?" It includes your assets as well as your limitations. The inventory is not a set of exams you have to pass in order to get a good grade in recovery. It is something you can do gently, at your own pace, coming back to it throughout your life as you grow to understand yourself better.

The fearlessness this Step asks for is not a lack of fear. If you wait until you feel no fear, you'll probably never begin your inventory! What you need for this Step is courage. The word *courage* comes from the Latin word for heart. *Courage* means "strength of heart." It means feeling fear but acting from the heart, not letting the fear immobilize you. In this chapter, you'll get to look at your fears about an inventory square in the face, decide which are realistic and which are not, and then move forward to act from the heart on this journey of self-discovery.

Fearlessness

1. What goes through your mind when you think about taking an inventory of yourself?

2. Read what you wrote under question 1. Do you see any realistic concerns? If so, what actions can you take to respond to those concerns?

    EXAMPLE:

    Instead of trying to plow through my inventory in one sitting, I need to work on it a little each week right before I go to a meeting where I have friends.

> My sponsor would say, "I hear a lot of guilt here. I don't think you're ready." And she was right. I wanted to get it over with because I felt so guilty. I was afraid of what would happen if I *didn't* do my inventory. It was really better to wait and walk through that fear.
>
> — GRETCHEN —

3. Now look again at what you wrote in question 1. Do you see any unrealistic fears? If so, circle them. Then practice the Third Step and turn those fears over to your Higher Power. You could even say something aloud like, "I am taking my fear of finding out how terrible I am and turning it over to my Higher Power. I am receiving from my Higher Power the serenity to accept things about myself that I can't change (like my past) and the courage to change the things I can."

Inventory

> The more we know about ourselves—our personal history, feelings, motivations, behaviors, and attitudes—the less likely we are to go back to drinking, using, overspending, or bingeing.
>
> — *A Woman's Way through the Twelve Steps*, page 68 —

4. There are many ways to do an inventory; this is your chance to try out one way. The next two pages are divided into two columns: Assets/strengths and Challenges/limitations. The words *deficit* and *weakness* are avoided because some women have a tendency to be self-critical and self-blaming.

In each column you'll see sentences that may or may not be true for you. Circle all the ones you think are true for you. Then add to both lists any other assets or challenges you can think of. You'll notice that the lists are divided into three sections: behaviors, feelings, and beliefs. Try to add at least a few words and/or sentences to each section. If you created an upward spiral in group, you can add some of the assets you wrote on it.

> I would find myself writing something and saying,
> "I don't want that to be true." It was painful to recognize
> parts of myself that I had never really faced.
>
> — SHANNON —

My Inventory: Behaviors

Assets/strengths	Challenges/limitations
I'm honest with myself about my strengths and limitations.	I have trouble recognizing my strengths.
I have discovered ways of surviving some very painful experiences.	I make excuses for others or myself.
I listen well to others.	I try to manipulate people rather than directly ask for what I want.
I don't use people.	I act before thinking about the consequences.
I stand up for myself.	I refuse to admit when I'm wrong.
I practice safe sex.	I don't ask for what I need—I don't want to bother people.
I keep my promises.	I isolate myself from people who care about me.
I don't take out my anger and frustration harshly on anyone.	I lie or deliberately deceive people.
I work hard to follow through on my commitments.	I demand perfection in myself and others.
I listen to my body and rest when I need to.	

My Inventory: Feelings

Assets/strengths	Challenges/limitations
I love my pet.	I fear admitting my limitations.
I'm really happy to be in recovery.	I get mad easily.
I'm more hopeful than I used to be.	Depression immobilizes me.
I feel calm under pressure.	I fear deep relationships.
I'm beginning to feel gratitude.	I feel misunderstood.
Passion is coming back in my sex life.	Sadness often overwhelms me.
I feel joyful for the first time in my life.	I worry constantly.

My Inventory: Beliefs

Assets/strengths	Challenges/limitations
My body is worth valuing.	My body is not worth valuing.
My Higher Power is trustworthy.	I need to compare my successes and failures to other people's.
I can live without the partner who was bad for me.	I'm to blame for what goes wrong.
Other people's needs matter.	I must get back at people who hurt me.
It's important to be fair.	I must be attractive at all times.
It's important to be honest.	What I want isn't that important.
My commitment to my loved ones is central in my life.	I'm inadequate.

Down the road, as I got on with understanding, I did another Fourth Step. I made a conscious effort to look at where I had participated in the things going on in my life. I saw that I had lied, cheated, stolen, manipulated, conned, beaten, bullied, been aggressive—I mean, what a list! I could simply own the behaviors, not judge whether I was right or wrong. With the nurturing and the validation I got, I could see which part needed healing and which needed changing.

— SHIRLEY —

Self-Soothing: "So What?"

Courage is acting from your heart, without letting fear stop you. One way to cultivate courage is to say, out loud:

"So what?"

Choose one of your fears that bothers you and write it in the space below.

EXAMPLE:

I'm afraid I'll fall apart if I face how hurt I was when my mother died.

Then in the space below, write "So what?" Say it out loud. Then write as much responding to "So what?" as you can think of.

> **EXAMPLE:**
>
> *So what if I fall apart? Lots of people fall apart in recovery. Maybe falling apart is a step toward putting my life together in a better way. So what if my family feels uncomfortable when I fall apart? It might be good for them. My friends in recovery will still love me.*

You might want to write "So what?" on a card and keep it in view while you write your inventory.

Gratitude

Write down one thing you've gained from working on Step Four that you're grateful for.

> **EXAMPLES:**
>
> *I've learned some things about myself.*
>
> *I've done something courageous.*

STEP FIVE

*Admitted to God, to ourselves, and to another
human being the exact nature of our wrongs.*

Step Five is about *admitting* and *naming* the truth about ourselves. As in Step Four, it is important for us to identify our strengths, not just our "wrongs" or limitations. And having identified these patterns of behavior, we put words to them that we speak aloud.

Many women fear that admitting the truth about themselves will lead to humiliation and rejection. After all, our society is prejudiced against women and gender-expansive people, especially those with addictive disorders. What, then, will others think of us when they know the things we feel ashamed of, perhaps our drinking, our sexual behavior, or our parenting? Surprisingly, though, when we act courageously and do Step Five, we usually find that putting an end to secrecy leads to connection rather than isolation—connection to ourselves, another person, and our Higher Power. Step Five brings us to self-acceptance and forgiveness, not guilt.

Naming our past experiences both honors them and gives us new perspectives on them. These new perspectives lead us to new options for acting differently in the future. In telling our story to another person, we often learn we're not the only ones in the universe who have felt or done such things. We also learn that others, too, have been able to make healthy changes.

There is no one right way to do Step Five. In this chapter, you will plan your Fifth Step in a way that feels safe and right for you.

Admitting

1. What goes through your mind when you think about telling another person the truth about your strengths and limitations?

2. It's important to use care in choosing the person to whom you will tell your story. Some qualities to look for in this person include:

   • an understanding of what you're trying to accomplish in Step Five

   • respect for your privacy and confidentiality

   • the ability to listen attentively

   • the ability to be emotionally present when you express fear, pain, tears, or laughter

   • openness to you as a person

   • the ability to hear what you say without being personally hurt by it

   In addition to these qualities, what else will you look for in the person who will hear your Fifth Step? (You may also want to put the above qualities into your own words so you're clear on what you want.)

   • _____

   • _____

   • _____

3. Who in your life possesses these qualities? (Consider your sponsor, a potential sponsor, a therapist, a friend, a minister, rabbi, priest, or spiritual advisor, etc.)

4. You may decide to share different parts of your story with different people. If you choose to do this, first ask yourself:

   • Am I telling different people in order to leave some parts of my story out altogether?

   • Am I telling different people because I believe there's no one who can hear my whole story and still accept me?

   If the answer to either of these questions is yes, your plan for doing your Fifth Step could end up increasing your secrecy and isolation. Because that's the opposite of the Step's purpose, you may want to reconsider your plan. The important thing with Step Five is to share it all—to leave nothing out.

   If you decide to do your Fifth Step with different people, how can you do this without reinforcing your secrecy and isolation?

5. There are many ways to do a Fifth Step. You may want to read aloud your Fourth Step, summarize your Fourth Step, or just tell stories from your life. You can do your whole Fifth Step in one sitting, or if that feels too stressful, you can break it into shorter pieces. You may decide to get as far as you can in an hour, and then take time to relax, reflect on the experience, and decide when to resume.

   How would you like to go about doing your Fifth Step? What format seems right for you and will help you get the most out of it?

6. If you're not sure how you want to do your Fifth Step, consider asking how others have done it. List the names of some people you know who have done Fifth Steps.

   _____

   _____

   _____

> Many women are all too ready to leap into a searching and fearless moral inventory with harsh judgment, looking only for negatives. As women we are constantly told about our defects of character, so we're very good at acknowledging our defects. We don't often hold other people accountable yet will hold ourselves over-accountable, taking all the responsibility and blame upon ourselves. . . . It is hard for us to say what's good about ourselves, what our assets are. A key piece of rediscovering our selves is also to name what is good about us.
>
> — JULIA —

Naming

7. Look back at the Assets/strengths and Challenges/limitations you listed under question 4 of Step Four (pages 36 and 37). Can you see any patterns of behavior that run through your life? Choose one behavior pattern that you would like to avoid repeating in the future. Name that behavior pattern here.

    EXAMPLES:

    I have often manipulated people to get what I want.

    Sometimes I get enraged and overreact when my children don't follow my directions.

8. Write a story about a time when you did this.

9. Now choose a behavior in your life that you like—something that feels successful, that you want to continue doing. (It could even be something you have done only once.) What is one thing you want to keep doing?

   EXAMPLE:

   I want to continue being honest with my friends.

10. Write a story about a time when you did this.

> Developing this kind of self-acceptance and self-forgiveness is really an art that you can learn. And once you do, once you practice the art of having compassion for yourself, you open yourself to one of the great promises of recovery outlined in the Big Book: "We will not regret the past nor wish to shut the door on it."[1]
>
> — *A Woman's Way through the Twelve Steps,* page 106 —

Developing a Loving Voice

Sometimes when we do Step Five, we focus on the things we don't like about ourselves. To maintain your balance as you work through this Step, practice using a loving voice when you talk to yourself.

11. Write three critical messages you often give yourself. Then imagine what a gentle, loving presence would say and write three of those messages.

Critical messages you give yourself	What a gentle, loving presence would say

12. What is the difference you feel when you use a loving voice instead of a critical voice?

Self-Soothing: Celebrate

Plan something fun for yourself after you've done your Fifth Step—or after the first piece of your Fifth Step, if you're going to break it up into several sessions. Plan something that will feel special, a celebration. Go to dinner with a friend. Go to a funny movie. Lie in the bathtub with candles lit. Turn on some joyful music and dance. Prepare a favorite food. What would be a great way for *you* to celebrate? Let yourself enjoy planning and looking forward to this time of fun. Enlist a friend's help, if you like. People in your recovery group will probably be eager to recognize this important event in your recovery.

Gratitude

Write down one thing you've gained from working on Step Five that you're grateful for.

EXAMPLES:

I have much less shame about my past.

I feel deeply accepted by my sponsor.

STEP SIX

*Were entirely ready to have God remove
all these defects of character.*

Readiness and *personal knowledge* are the themes of Step Six. This Step does not demand that we change right now; rather, it invites us to become ready to change. Readiness is willingness—willingness to let go of habits or traits that have unbalanced our lives. Readiness may even be the willingness to become willing. Perhaps we're not yet ready to change, but we're ready to be open to the possibility of change.

A key part of this readiness is openness to a deeper knowledge of ourselves. Most of us need to become aware of a behavior pattern, then spend some time working with that awareness before we're ready to change the pattern. That's the way it was with our addiction: it took time for us to become aware that we had an addiction, then more time before we accepted it and became willing to let go of the destructive behavior. We need time to recognize the barriers that keep us from changing our behavior. Step Six, then, is not something we do all at once, but a process we enter into over and over throughout our lives.

In this chapter, you'll practice some concrete rituals that represent what it means to let go. You'll also focus on one pattern that you want to change and examine the barriers that have been keeping you from letting go of it.

Readiness

1. Doing something symbolic can help you learn with your body what it means to become ready to let go of something. Choose or adapt one of the following things to do:

    • If you live near an ocean, a lake, a pond, or a river, gather twelve stones and throw them into the water, one at a time. (You could also do this with twelve pennies and a fountain, or twelve pennies or stones and a bucket of water; if you don't have those items, you could also do this activity with twelve handfuls of water in a sink.) The point is to feel yourself either hurling the stones or pennies into the water with all your might or gently opening your hand to let the stones or pennies drop into the water. Gentle or fierce—do what your body seems to want to do. As you let go of the stones, say to yourself, "I'm letting go of . . ."

    • Gather twelve leaves and release them into the breeze. You could drop them out of a second-story window (or from any high place) and watch them blow away. You could stand on the ground and throw them into the air. This will work best if you throw them all at once. As you let go of the leaves, say to yourself, "I'm letting go of . . ."

2. What was it like for you to do this letting-go ritual?

3. Look back at the behaviors and beliefs you wrote in question 4 of Step Four (pages 36 and 37). Choose two or three that you would like to let go of. Write them on small pieces of paper. Then, do one of the following:

    • Flush the pieces of paper down a toilet.

    • Put the pieces of paper in a flameproof container (an ashtray or a casserole dish or outdoor grill) and burn them.

    • Shred the pieces using a paper shredder.

    • Tear the papers into tiny pieces and throw them into the trash.

4. What are the behaviors or beliefs you chose to release?

    _____

    _____

    _____

5. What did you learn about being ready (willing) to let go?

"We claim spiritual progress rather than spiritual perfection."[1]
In other words, you can focus on your progress and accept
that you are *im*perfect, *un*willing, and *not* ready.

— *A Woman's Way through the Twelve Steps*, page 117 —

Personal Knowledge

Look back at your answers to questions 7 and 8 of Step Five (pages 44 and 45). In those questions, you wrote about a behavior pattern that you want to stop repeating. If that behavior still feels like a priority for you, focus on it in the questions below. If you see another behavior in yourself that seems like more of a priority, you can focus on that one instead. The examples below will be explored throughout Steps Six and Seven to help you think about your own process.

6. Name the behavior pattern or quality that you want to have removed.

    EXAMPLES:

    a. *I have often manipulated people to get what I want.*

    b. *Sometimes I get enraged and overreact when my children don't follow my directions.*

7. Sometimes we are completely responsible for a pattern of behavior. For example, it's never appropriate to call someone names.

    On the other hand, especially in relationships with other people, there are sometimes parts of a pattern that we are *not* responsible for. We are not responsible for what someone else does. It's helpful to figure out which things are our responsibility and which things aren't.

    Are there any aspects of the behavior pattern you named in question 6 that you are not responsible for? If so, what are those aspects?

EXAMPLES:

a. *When I ask people directly for something I need, they often ignore me. So I've learned to be manipulative. I'm not responsible for the fact that people ignore my direct requests.*

b. *I'm not responsible for my children's decisions not to follow my guidance.*

8. What *are* you responsible for in the pattern you have chosen to write about? (You are responsible for your own feelings and behavior.)

    EXAMPLES:

a. *I choose to manipulate my boss rather than say what I think directly and respectfully. I have been afraid of getting in trouble with my boss if I acted straightforwardly and assertively.*

b. *My anger erupts because I feel frustrated. I am responsible for any harm I do when I'm angry. I am responsible for learning to cope when my children don't listen. I am responsible for earning my children's respect so they will do what I ask without being afraid of my anger.*

> My body and mind may hold on to old patterns,
> even though I'm ready to start new ones. . . . Step Six
> reminds me that I am always a work in progress.
>
> — ESSIE —

9. What are the barriers that have been keeping you from changing your particular behavior? For instance:

- What do you fear might happen if you let go of this behavior?
- How does this behavior protect you from pain?
- What feeling does this behavior help you avoid?

EXAMPLES:

a. *I don't know any other way to get what I want. If I don't manipulate people, I might never get what I need from them.*

b. *I'm afraid my children might hurt themselves or others if I don't control their behavior. I don't know how to get them to listen to me without getting angry. Rage helps me avoid feeling helpless or vulnerable.*

Exploring Values

10. Instructions: fill in your own answers to the statements that follow.

I spend most of my time _____

_____ .

My favorite thing to do is _____

_____ .

I would like to be able to _____

_____ .

I want to be seen as _____

_____ .

People should _____

_____ .

People should not _____

_____ .

What is most important to me is _____

_____ .

My greatest fear is _____

_____ .

My greatest achievement is _____

_____. ☐

My greatest strength is _____

_____. ☐

What do I stand for? I stand for _____

_____. ☐

Whom do I stand with? I share beliefs and values with _____

_____. ☐

Next, rank each of these statements, by putting a number next to it, according to how strongly you feel about it:

Rank it 1 if you feel very strongly about it.

Rank it 2 if you feel relatively strongly about it.

Rank it 3 if you feel that it is mildly important.

Rank it 4 if you feel that it is not really important.

When you identify your values, you may discover that there's a behavior you want to change in order to live more consistently with your values.

Self-Soothing: Journaling

Feelings like fear and vulnerability can seem too big to handle. When emotions feel big, it often helps to write them down. Writing helps us process what we're really feeling, what's causing those feelings, and whether or how we want to act on them. Writing can help us make sense of a confusing or painful experience also. We can rant and rave on paper instead of raging out loud at people.

Writing is a good way to examine positive feelings and experiences as well. Many of us carry our painful moments around as heavy burdens but quickly forget life's joys and successes. If we put those joys into words on paper, we can read them and relive them anytime we need a lift.

A journal is a book in which you can write down things like this. It's a private place to write about your experiences, thoughts, and feelings. There are no rules about how a journal should look: a spiral notebook, a three-ring binder, or a beautifully bound little book are some options. Some people find it easier and more comfortable to write in a notebook that can lie flat. There are no rules about how often you write in your journal or about grammar, spelling, or anything else. You can jot notes, make lists, sketch, doodle—whatever feels helpful.

Buy or put together a journal for yourself. If you are taking notes at Twelve Step meetings in your own Little Book, you can use that notebook, or you can start a new book. At the top of the first page, write today's date. Take about twenty minutes to write down either (a) something you learned today or (b) something that happened today. Include your feelings about the insight or experience. What did you learn about yourself or others today? What is something you've come to believe? Don't worry about creating something profound or something that others will read. Scrawl or WRITE IN BIG LETTERS or draw. This is for you.

Gratitude

Write down one thing you've gained from working on Step Six that you're grateful for.

> **EXAMPLES:**
>
> *I'm more relaxed about the areas of my life in which I want to grow.*
>
> *I understand more about the barriers inside me that keep me from changing my behavior.*

STEP SEVEN

Humbly asked Him to remove our shortcomings.

Step Seven helps us learn about the concepts of *relinquishment* and *humility*. It's important to understand that the humility of Step Seven is not humiliation. True humility means having a strong sense of who we are—realizing our limitations and acknowledging our strengths. Humility doesn't mean being passive or embarrassed about ourselves. It means acknowledging both our mistakes and our successes, not puffing ourselves up or squashing ourselves down, and moving forward to do what we need to do the next time. Humility also includes the knowledge that willpower alone won't change us. We couldn't force ourselves to break the pattern of our addiction by willpower, and we can't change any other pattern in that way either. We need to align ourselves with a Power greater than ourselves and allow the changes to come in their own time.

Relinquishment, the other concept in Step Seven, simply means letting go or turning things over to our Higher Power. It's cooperating with our Higher Power in the process of letting go. In Step Seven, we find that change involves a partnership between us and our Higher Power. There are many ways we can put into action our decision to cooperate—including (but not limited to) prayer. In this chapter, you'll experiment with a ritual that demonstrates how to turn something over to your Higher Power. You'll also think about concrete action you can take in the partnership of changing a behavior pattern.

Relinquishment

The partnership of Step Seven includes action you need to take and also a decision to accept help and guidance from your Higher Power. It's like singing a duet: you listen for the melody your Higher Power is singing, and you sing the harmony. *Listening for the melody* means aligning yourself with this force in the universe. Our *shortcomings* are the things that keep us from listening. As we turn them over, we are better able to hear the melody.

So what is involved in turning things over, or listening for the melody?

1. Turning something over to your Higher Power can seem abstract. A Surrender box or God box provides a concrete way of turning something over. If you didn't make a Surrender box in group, find a shoe box, a jewelry box, a coffee can, or a similar container. Even an envelope will work. Decorate it if you like or label it.

2. Look back at questions 6 through 9 of Step Six (pages 51–53). When you're ready to turn over the behavior pattern you wrote about in those questions, write a description of that pattern on a piece of paper and put it in your Surrender box or God box. Remember that you can always change your mind and take the paper out again. Putting the paper in means you are turning control over to your Higher Power. Taking the paper out means you are taking control back.

3. You can also put descriptions or symbols of other things you want to turn over into your box. You can add the names of people, places, or things you've been trying to control. Anything you don't want to carry anymore—write it down and put it in the box. Then shut the lid or close the flap.

4. What was it like for you to make a Surrender box? How did you feel when you put something into it?

5. Was the process helpful? Meaningless?

6. Did it produce a mixture of feelings? Which feelings?

7. Step Seven speaks of "asking" your Higher Power to do something with the things you've turned over. You may think of asking as a prayer or as an openness to receive help and guidance. Think about one specific thing you wrote down and put into your God box or Surrender box. What are you open to receiving from your Higher Power? Or what would you like to ask of your Higher Power?

OPTIONAL PROJECT

Write your own Seventh Step prayer or request. How would you ask your Higher Power or Inner Spirit to remove the behavior patterns that don't serve you well?

Humility

Using the Surrender box or God box is one way of turning things over, of "listening to the melody." The second part of the duet involves action: singing the harmony. You're taking action, but not in isolation. Part of humility is recognizing that we can't recover alone; we do it in partnership with others and our Higher Power. It's still a duet—you're aligning yourself with what your Higher Power is singing. So now let's think about your side of the partnership, the harmony you're going to sing.

8. Look again at your answers to questions 6 through 9 of Step Six (pages 51–53). What action do you need to take in order to cooperate with your Higher Power in changing this pattern?

    EXAMPLES:

    a. *I'm going to talk to my sponsor about how to ask my boss directly for something I need, and the fear I feel when I do. I'm going to practice a conversation with my sponsor in which I tell my boss, "I have some questions about exactly what you're looking for in this task I'm doing. When would be a good time to discuss this project in more detail?"*

    b. *I need to learn some calming techniques to use when I start feeling angry at my children. I will research and practice techniques that work for me.*

> Humility also means I recognize a spiritual
> source greater than myself.
>
> — ELENA —

9. What feelings do you have when you think about taking the action you've just described?

   EXAMPLES:

   a. *I feel scared, but I also feel proud of myself that I have a plan for taking action. Talking to my sponsor feels like a good first step toward change that doesn't put pressure on me to change all at once.*

   b. *I'm relieved that there's something I can do to improve my relationship with my children.*

10. Because humility means acknowledging our strengths as well as our mistakes, it's a good idea to look at the behavior we are turning over and think also about its hidden strengths that we don't want to lose.

Is there anything in the behavior pattern you've been writing about that you want to keep? Anything that works for you without harming someone else? If so, describe what you want to keep. If not, feel free to say so!

EXAMPLES:

a. *When I manipulated my boss, I learned to read her well. I don't want to lose that ability.*

b. *It can feel good in the moment to let out my anger, but I want to remember that in the long run, I don't want my kids to be scared. I can still feel anger but express it clearly, directly, and concisely without harming anyone.*

My mistakes are simply my mistakes;
they don't *define* me anymore.

— *A Woman's Way through the Twelve Steps*, page 123 —

Self-Soothing: Palms Down, Palms Up

A technique called Palms Down, Palms Up can help you practice turning things over each day.

> Sit comfortably with your back straight. Close or lower your eyes and focus on your breathing. Take a slow, deep breath while counting to four. Then exhale slowly, counting to four. Do this four more times until your breathing is slow and relaxed.
>
> Keep breathing slowly and evenly. Place your hands gently in front of you with the palms down. Imagine yourself emptying your hands of everything you've been carrying today. Your hands are empty of people, things, and situations. They are empty of behaviors you want to let go of. They are also empty of trying to let go of those behaviors. They are just empty, palms down.
>
> Now, turn your palms up. Keep breathing slowly. Your palms are up, open to receive whatever your Higher Power sends to you. You are open to receive what you need to live today. Your palms are open to help.
>
> Anytime during the day when you need to let go of something and receive help, you can take a few minutes to do the Palms Down, Palms Up exercise.

Gratitude

Write down one thing you've gained from working on Step Seven that you're grateful for.

EXAMPLES:

I feel lighter after turning over some heavy things.

I have a plan for making change in an area where I've felt stuck.

STEP EIGHT

Made a list of all persons we had harmed, and became willing to make amends to them all.

In the earlier Steps we looked to see where our own lives were out of balance. Now we focus on imbalances in our relationships: with family, friends, partners, former partners, neighbors, employers, co-workers, ministers, teachers, government officials, cashiers, mechanics—anyone. Step Eight helps us learn to use two relationship tools: *discernment* and *willingness*.

First, we sort out how our actions have affected others and what we can do to set our relationships right. We decide what we are responsible for as well as what others are responsible for. We learn to see the harm without condemning ourselves.

Second, we open our minds to the possibility of making amends. We don't need to make amends yet. (That will happen in Step Nine.) We simply explore the possibility and address any barriers that keep us from being willing.

In this chapter, you will make a short list of people you feel you have harmed. You'll also think about what (if anything) keeps you from being willing to make amends to them.

Discernment

Discernment is about telling the difference between one thing and another. In recovery we begin to sort out the people we have harmed and the people we haven't. A list of a hundred people you've harmed throughout your life is not usually helpful for your first work on Step Eight. As you do the exercises in this chapter, remember that you can always come back to Step Eight later for a deeper look at your past.

1. Make a list of four or five people you've harmed within the past few years. Think especially of people you've harmed as a result of your addiction—perhaps while using a substance or while protecting your supply. Be sure to include yourself on that list. Below are some questions to spark your thinking:

    - In which of my relationships is there bitterness, fear, or hostility?

    - Whom do I resent or avoid?

    - In what relationships have I left unfinished business?

    - Whom do I want to treat differently from now on?

    - With whom do I want to be more honest?

    - Am I unhappy with anyone but afraid to tell them?

    - Am I trying to control any of my relationships?

2. On the next three pages, you'll have a chance to think through these relationships. You'll write down:

    - *Name:* The person's name.

    - *Your responsibility:* How have you harmed this person? List some specific actions—words, tones of voice, things you didn't do that you should have done—and how your actions affected the other person. Remember to take responsibility only for *your* actions, not for things that are really the other person's responsibility. The other person also may have done things to hurt you, but this isn't the place to get into that side of the story.

    - *Your feelings:* What hurt, sadness, anger, fear, guilt, or shame do you feel about this relationship? Do you feel any joy, excitement, hope, or love?

    - *Your intentions:* What do you hope to accomplish by making amends or telling the truth?

a. Name: _____

 • Your responsibility:

 • Your feelings:

 • Your intentions:

b. Name: _____

 • Your responsibility:

 • Your feelings:

 • Your intentions:

c. Name: _____

  • Your responsibility:

  • Your feelings:

  • Your intentions:

d. Name: _____

  • Your responsibility:

  • Your feelings:

  • Your intentions:

e. Name: _____

• Your responsibility:

• Your feelings:

• Your intentions:

Willingness

3. In Step Nine, you'll decide what you can do to make amends to these people. For now, just think about barriers. What is keeping you from being willing to make amends to each person you've named?

> **EXAMPLES:**
>
> *I'm afraid she'll lose respect for me.*
>
> *I'm afraid he'll get angry and yell.*
>
> *I don't have the money.*
>
> *I just need to live with the fact that this relationship is over.*
>
> *Thinking about talking with them makes me feel so uncomfortable.*

a. Name: _____

  • Barriers to making amends:

b. Name: _____

  • Barriers to making amends:

c. Name: _____

  • Barriers to making amends:

d. Name: _____

  • Barriers to making amends:

e. Name: _____

  • Barriers to making amends:

> Today, because I love myself enough, I put my best self forward by
> being honest with myself—with what's really going on with me.
> "To thine own self be true." I try to do this in all my relationships.
> What I need to do is be direct and honest about what's going on
> with me and let other people deal with it as they choose.
>
> — JACKIE —

Planting Seeds

When we plant seeds and watch the seeds sprout, we can see some parallels with what we learn in Step Eight:

- We are responsible for our efforts but cannot control the results. We have planted, watered, and placed these cups in the sunlight. But the actual growth of the seeds is something we can't control.

- Very few things in life are perfect. All the cups are different, and even if the seeds sprout, few of the plants are perfect.

- Still, growing is necessary for life. Much of life is out of our control, but we still need to try to do our best. There is a saying in AA: "We are responsible for the efforts but not the results."

- Our recovery is like the seeds in the cups: it does not grow and develop on its own. It needs watchfulness and tending. Sometimes people forget to nurture their recoveries. We do need to make the effort to maintain the changes we have made in our lives.

4. List any other principles you learned from planting and tending seeds.

Visualizing Good Relationships

5. Think about the best relationship you've had with another person or imagine an ideal relationship. Describe what you like about that person, how you feel when you're with them, and how you act in the relationship.

Describe what you see about yourself and what you want in relationships.

Creating a Joy List

6. List ten things in your life that bring you joy:

1. _____

2. _____

3. _____

4. _____

5. _____

6. _____

7. _____

8. _____

9. _____

10. _____

Self-Soothing: Movement

Sometimes the best way to get anxiety, stress, guilt, or loneliness out of our bodies is to do something that gets our bodies moving. What kind of physical activity do you enjoy? What relaxes you or lifts your mood? You could:

- dance (move to music slowly and gracefully—or wildly and enthusiastically)

- run

- walk

- rock in a chair or on the floor

- lift weights

If you feel embarrassed moving in front of other people, find a private place and twirl or leap or do chorus-line kicks. Pretend you're a bird and glide around the room with your arms out. Forget about how you look—no one's watching!

Gratitude

Write down one thing you've gained from working on Step Eight that you're grateful for.

EXAMPLES:

I'm starting to believe I might actually be able to unload the guilt I've been carrying around.

I realize that I've harmed myself, and recovery is part of making amends to myself.

STEP NINE

*Made direct amends to such people wherever possible,
except when to do so would injure them or others.*

When we do Step Nine, we need to understand two things: what it means to make *amends* and what *action* we need to take in each relationship. *Making amends* means taking responsibility for your part in a relationship. *Taking responsibility* means responding appropriately to the other person. You spent time in Step Eight distinguishing your part from the other person's part in each relationship. Now you're ready to think about what action would be an appropriate response in each case.

In most cases, direct and honest amends involve a spoken apology or some direct action, such as repaying money. Sometimes, though, it's more appropriate to make "living" amends—to start treating someone with more kindness or respect, for example. If we can't go directly to someone (if the person has died, for example), we can make "symbolic" amends, such as giving money to charity or writing a letter to read to our sponsor.

In this chapter, you'll decide how to make amends to each person you listed in Step Eight. You'll consider responding in ways that are appropriate and don't injure anyone, and you'll examine your motives and let go of the outcome.

Amends

1. Look back at what you wrote in questions 1 and 2 of Step Eight (pages 65–68). Before you decide on the action you want to take as amends for each person, pause to think about your motives. Your motive is your reason or intention for doing something. For each person on your list, *why* do you want to make amends? For example, are you:

- trying to control a relationship by taking the blame?

- trying to gain acceptance or keep someone from abandoning you?

- hoping that person will feel guilty or make amends to you in return?

- intending to vent your anger through an apology?

- trying to get the person to respond in a certain way?

- genuinely aiming to make things right?

- hoping to improve the relationship?

- dealing responsibly with guilt?

For each person on your list, write down your motive for making amends.

a. Name: _____

- Motive:

b. Name: _____

- Motive:

c. Name: _____

   • Motive:

d. Name: _____

   • Motive:

e. Name: _____

   • Motive:

2. If you have any mixed motives for making amends that you need to let go of, circle them in the list you made. How could you think about the situation differently? What do you need to do differently?

    EXAMPLES:

    I need to let go of my desire to control this person's response to me.

    I need to wait to make amends until I've found a constructive way to deal with my anger.

3. When you think about the fact that you have *no control over the other person's response* to your amends, how do you feel? (Anxious? Relieved? Content? Frustrated?)

Honesty without sensitivity is brutality.

— *A Woman's Way through the Twelve Steps,* page 160 —

Action

4. What do you need to do to create the best possible relationship with each person on your list? Remember to think of your part in the relationship and not to take responsibility for the other person's part.

    EXAMPLES:

    Direct amends: Apologize and ask for forgiveness without making any jabs about the other person's behavior.

    Direct amends: Pay her the money I owe her.

    Direct amends to myself: Get enough rest each night.

    Living amends: Say nothing but start treating her more respectfully.

    Living amends: Be honest with him about what I'm feeling.

    Living amends: Commit to spending two hours a week interacting with my daughter in an activity she enjoys.

    Symbolic amends: Make a donation to the college where I cheated on tests.

    Symbolic amends: Plant a tree because I ran into a tree with my car when I was high.

    a. Name: _____

      • Amends:

    b. Name: _____

      • Amends:

c. Name: _____

• Amends:

d. Name: _____

• Amends:

e. Name: _____

• Amends:

5. Look back over your list of amends to be sure these actions won't injure you, the other person, or someone else. If you think someone might be injured, change your plan. Remember that making yourself uncomfortable or sparking the other person's anger is not necessarily injury. Some discomfort, hurt feelings, or anger may be part of the process of clearing the air. You may want to talk with your sponsor or someone else you trust about your plans and whether they'll really cause injury. (Remember to add yourself to this list.)

> In every situation, I now respond, rather than react. That
> means taking the time to think a situation through and
> make a decision about the best possible response.
>
> — MARTA —

6. Follow through with your plan for amends to at least one person. Afterward, write here about the experience. What are you feeling? What have you learned?

> I tend to want everyone to like me. I had to learn that not everyone
> will be able to be your friend, when I did my Ninth Step.
>
> — RAQUELLE —

Self-Soothing: A Peaceful Place

We all need a place to go to be protected from stress for a while. Sometimes, though, we can't easily go to a real-world refuge. For those times, it helps to have a special place in our minds.

To find your peaceful place, begin by taking a slow, deep breath. Close or lower your eyes and keep breathing slowly and deeply. Let your body relax with each breath.

When your body starts to feel heavy, let your imagination wander to a place that feels relaxed and safe. It could be a real place you've been to or a place you imagine. It may be outdoors or indoors: a room, a meadow, a beach, a garden. Imagine it just the way you like it: with people or without, in bright or dim light, warmer or cooler. Lock the door of this place or build high walls if they make you feel safer. Or open the space up if you need room to breathe.

Next, imagine yourself sitting or lying comfortably in this soothing place. Imagine peaceful sounds, perhaps a relaxing fragrance. Let the soothing place soak into your body.

You can learn to go to your peaceful place with ease by practicing this: Close your eyes and go to your peaceful place for a minute. Then open your eyes and return to the real world. Then close your eyes again and go to your peaceful place. Practice going back and forth several times until going there seems natural.

Gratitude

Write down one thing you've gained from working on Step Nine that you're grateful for.

> **EXAMPLES:**
>
> *I've set my relationship with my mother on a much better track.*
>
> *I'm no longer embarrassed to walk into the store where I shoplifted.*

STEP TEN

Continued to take personal inventory and when we were wrong promptly admitted it.

Step Ten is the first of the three maintenance Steps, helping you maintain the gains you have made. Having done Steps Four through Nine, we already know how to do Step Ten. In this Step, we simply commit to the regular practices of taking inventory and acknowledging our mistakes, practices that were so beneficial in earlier Steps. This regular practice—call it a check-in or "putting the day to bed"—is a *discipline* that builds emotional and spiritual health. Spiritual practice is the process of turning again and again to a discipline or task, and doing it even when we appear to be going nowhere. The point is to bring ourselves into harmony with the essence of life in the present moment and to express it in all our affairs.

While earlier Steps dealt with the past, Step Ten helps us *stay present*. We check in with ourselves on how our present relationships and emotions are doing. We make amends right away, before things have a chance to slide downhill.

In this chapter, you'll sample one way of practicing a regular check-in with yourself in order to find your own consistent way of doing Step Ten.

Staying Present

One way of practicing Step Ten is called "putting the day to bed." Each night before you go to bed, you review your day. You ask yourself questions like:

- What did I notice today about myself or others?
- What strengths did I show today?

- What were my challenges today?

- Have I been dishonest with myself or someone else today?

- How did I feel about myself today?

- Is there any unfinished business between me and someone else?

- What am I grateful for today?

1. For the next four or five days, set aside twenty minutes each evening to "put the day to bed." Think about your day—the questions above may help. Then ask yourself if there's anything you need to do to set things right. It's important to take some time for reflection in our busy lives. This is not just a diary of the bare events that happened, but a look below the surface at what things meant to us. Below and on the following pages, write your thoughts about your day for the next five days.

Day 1:

What can I do to set things right?

Day 2:

What can I do to set things right?

Day 3:

What can I do to set things right?

Day 4:

What can I do to set things right?

Day 5:

What can I do to set things right?

> Whether it's washing dishes, gardening, or meditating,
> it is about staying in this place. Practice forces us to
> live more fully in the present moment.
>
> — RUTH —

Discipline

After you've practiced putting your day to bed for several days, use the following questions to reflect on the experience.

2. What did you learn about yourself from reviewing your day?

3. What barriers make it challenging for you to maintain a regular practice of thinking about each day?

4. How can you overcome those barriers? What will a regular Step Ten practice look like for you?

If you'd like to, you can use the journal you started in Step Six to continue the practice of putting your day to bed.

I continue to take a personal inventory of my truth and promptly admit it, no matter what I find. Go deeper with the truth and always honor it, even if it feels uncomfortable or difficult.

— JACKIE —

Transformation Visualization

5. Sit comfortably, lower your eyes, and focus on your breathing for a few moments. Then think about a behavior pattern or quality you'd like to change. Write a description of the pattern's characteristics, what it looks like, and what it feels like.

6. Then think about what the opposite of this pattern would be for you. Write a description of its characteristics, what it looks like, and what it feels like.

7. If you did this visualization in group, draw the symbol you received during it. Show what the transformation you seek looks like—and remember to *act as if*.

Loving Yourself

8. List all the things you can think of that you love about yourself. Your list might include the kind of friend you are, how you treat your coworkers, your creativity, how your body works, how you act when you're sober. Enjoy exploring what you love about yourself as you make your list.

_____   _____

_____   _____

_____   _____

_____   _____

_____   _____

_____   _____

_____   _____

_____   _____

9. Next, write two positive affirmations that you'd like to repeat to yourself this week.

_____

_____

Self-Soothing: Walking Meditation

Some forms of meditation help us become more aware of the present moment. One is walking meditation. Find a room or a safe place outdoors where you have a bit of open space to walk around and a few minutes to be alone and undisturbed. The outdoors is ideal, but you could also walk around inside your home. The idea in a walking meditation is to walk *very slowly*. It should take at least five seconds to take one step.

To begin, stand and take a slow, deep breath. Keep your eyes open and focused on the ground or the space in front of you. Take a very slow step. Feel every movement of every muscle. Feel the pressure of the ground when you set your foot down. Pause. Take another step. Notice any areas of tension in your body. Observe each feeling without judging it as good or bad. If distracting thoughts come to your mind, let them drain away gently as you focus on your body. Feel yourself setting your heel down, then the ball of your foot, and finally your toes. Pause. Then take another step.

Walk for about three to five minutes. You might set a timer so that you don't have to think about the time.

If walking is difficult for you, move your arms instead. Sit comfortably and begin by taking a slow, deep breath. Very slowly, move your arms up, then out, and back down to your lap. Feel the weight of your arms as they move slowly through the air. Repeat the movements several times, keeping the movements slow and smooth. Reverse the motion of your arms. Feel how your muscles move differently.

If it's comfortable, press your hands down by your sides and let your arms and shoulders take some of your weight for a few moments. Feel your palms push down, and notice the muscles in your arms, shoulders, and torso. Take a long breath, and slowly relax your arms.

Gratitude

Write down one thing you've gained from working on Step Ten that you're grateful for.

EXAMPLES:

Reviewing my day helped me recognize that I was feeling anxious and discover why. Then I did something about it.

I'm getting clearer and more confident about what I believe and value.

STEP ELEVEN

Sought through prayer and meditation to improve our conscious contact with God as we understood Him, praying only for knowledge of His will for us and the power to carry that out.

Prayer, meditation, and *conscious contact* are the themes of Step Eleven. In *A Woman's Way through the Twelve Steps, prayer* is defined as "an act of either reaching out to a Higher Power or going inward to a deeper knowing. Just as we described God in our own way in Step Three, we can also come to prayer however we like."[1] Some women find the prayers of AA helpful, others adapt the AA prayers to fit their understanding of God, and others find quite different ways of praying.

Similarly, there are many ways of thinking about conscious contact. We can think of it as spiritual awareness and connection, as a dialogue or attunement with the spirit moving in the universe, or as a choice to think and act in harmony with that spirit. Conscious contact is a deliberate choice to cooperate with our Higher Power. We open ourselves to possibilities that we don't control.

If prayer is reaching out to communicate, meditation is being still and *listening*. It is a time to surrender, to receive, to let go. A habit of meditation creates a peaceful place in us, no matter what dramas occur in our daily lives.

> Serenity is not freedom from the storms of life.
> It is the calm in the center that gets me through.
>
> — *A Woman's Way through the Twelve Steps*, page 193 —

"Listening" in meditation doesn't necessarily mean hearing something, yet the habit of listening is a way to build our openness to what life brings us.

Like Step Ten, Step Eleven is a maintenance Step in which you establish daily practices that will help you throughout your life. In this chapter, you will reflect on how you now see your Higher Power, and you'll experiment with some daily practices of conscious contact and spiritual awareness.

Prayer

1. Our understanding of our Higher Power often grows and changes as we move through recovery. Look back at what you wrote for questions 5 and 6 of Step Two (pages 18–19). How has your understanding of your Higher Power changed or stayed the same? What do you believe about your Higher Power now?

2. How do you pray? What would a regular habit of prayer look like for you?

   EXAMPLES:

   I say one of the AA prayers every morning.

   I have adapted or written my own daily prayer. It goes like this: . . .

   I take ten minutes before bed to talk to my Higher Power in whatever words come to me.

   In Islam, we pray five times a day. This is my favorite prayer . . .

You can find the Twelve Step Prayers, including the Serenity Prayer, on page 107 in the appendix.

> In prayer I am entering into a conversation. I'm asking aloud, "What
> do I need from the universe and what does it need from me?"
>
> — GRACE —

Meditation

3. Plan three to five minutes of daily meditation for the next four or five days. You may want to think ahead about when the best time of day for you is. The first or last minutes of the day work well for some people; other people are rushed or sleepy at those times. Can you go somewhere alone at lunchtime? Can you take an afternoon break? When is a good time of day for you to take three to five minutes of stillness?

4. You have already learned several methods of meditation for self-soothing. In Step Three, you learned about focusing on your breathing. In Step Seven, you learned Palms Down, Palms Up. In Step Ten, you learned about walking meditation.

    There are many other methods, but they all have a few things in common. The first is the position of your body. Unless you are doing a walking meditation, you will probably sit still to meditate. You can sit in a chair or on the floor. It's important to find a position that is comfortable enough that you won't need to shift around while you're meditating. It's also important to sit up with your spine straight and your head level over your spine. Sitting up straight tells your body to stay alert and focused. It's a helpful position for being relaxed and alert. Also, sitting up straight allows you to breathe deeply and freely. In this way, energy can move freely through your body. So find a position in which you won't slump or arch your back. If you need a pillow behind your back to support it, use one. Some people can comfortably sit on the floor with their backs straight and their legs crossed. Others like to kneel on the floor sitting on their heels with their backs straight. Do whatever helps you achieve these three goals:

    *   sitting still
    *   feeling comfortable
    *   having a straight spine

    For the next four or five days, practice three to five minutes of meditation. You can experiment with a variety of positions. Take a moment now to think about how you can sit still and comfortably with a straight spine when you meditate today.

5. It's usually a good idea to take a few slow, deep breaths before you begin a meditation. Just count to four while you inhale slowly; then count to four while you exhale. Doing that three or four times will help you relax and focus your mind.

After these slow breaths, you'll settle into your meditation. In the beginning, three to five minutes is enough. Eventually you may want to stretch the time to fifteen or twenty minutes, but don't rush yourself. You're not competing with anyone.

The idea in meditation is to be fully present, to open yourself up, and not to think about anything. You're listening, not mentally talking. You're letting your mind become quiet. The various forms of meditation are similar in that they are all designed to still your mind and focus your attention.

For example, you may want to sit with your eyes closed. If you do that, then you can focus your mind by concentrating on the breath going in and out of your nose. Or you can repeat a word or phrase over and over in your mind, slowly. Something simple is ideal: *peace, thank you, om* (a traditional contemplative word in Buddhism), or the name of your Higher Power. This word is simply a way to express your intention to be fully present to the spirit in the universe.

Other people prefer to have their eyes open and focused on an object. For instance, you can light a candle, place it on a table in front of you, and focus your eyes on the flame. Or you can set a flower on a table in front of you and focus your eyes on the flower. If you prefer an eyes-open meditation, the important thing is to focus your eyes on one thing, not to shift your gaze around. It's also helpful to choose something soothing like a candle or flower, or something that has spiritual meaning for you. For instance, a picture may have spiritual meaning for you. Or you might use a symbolic object, such as a Star of David or a cross.

Whether you close your eyes and focus on a word or open your eyes and focus on an object, the point is the same: to give your mind something to do while you let the busy thoughts drain out of it. Still, almost all of us have days when our minds refuse to settle down. When this happens, you can simply observe your mind having its thoughts. Observe the thoughts and let them go by. If you have emotions, observe the emotions and let them go by. If you get frustrated about "not doing it right," just observe the frustration and let it drift away gently.

When you meditate today, what word or object will you use to focus your mind?

6. Now that you've thought about when and how you'd like to meditate, do it for three to five minutes for the next four or five days.

> Whenever I'm faced with a challenge, I sit quietly and
> meditate, asking for help to get out of my own way.
> I ask for the strength to do what I'm here to do.
>
> — *A Woman's Way through the Twelve Steps,* page 195 —

Conscious Contact

7. How have prayer and meditation helped you increase your conscious contact with your Higher Power? Or how do you think prayer and meditation will be helpful over time?

> Prayer and meditation are like conversation, and that is how we
> improve our conscious contact. Prayer reminds me to reach out, to
> be in a position of asking for help. Prayer is action in relationship.
>
> — GRACE —

Support Groups

8. Fill in the blanks with people you can contact in the following situations. Put their contact information in your phone or your Little Book.

People I can call when I'm feeling down:

_____ _____ _____

People to call in a crisis:

_____ _____

People I can call when I feel like returning to use:

_____ _____ _____

People to call who inspire me to do what's good for me:

_____ _____

Self-Soothing: Self-Soothing Chart

By now you have sampled a variety of ways to comfort yourself without addictive behavior. The following chart can help you organize your ideas for soothing yourself; different methods of self-soothing are appropriate for different situations. It's helpful to think through what you can do to care for yourself in various situations so you won't have to think so hard when you're under stress. Some things will work when you are alone but not in a room full of people. You can do some methods during the day but not at night.

Take a few minutes to think of ideas for soothing yourself in each type of situation. Write your ideas in the self-soothing chart.

Self-Soothing Chart

	Alone	With others
Daytime	**EXAMPLES:** *take a walk, sit by a body of water, do breathing meditation*	**EXAMPLES:** *ask for a hug, recite affirmations silently to myself*
Nighttime	**EXAMPLES:** *write in my journal, take a hot bath*	**EXAMPLES:** *say, "So what?" to myself, go to my peaceful place in my mind for a minute or two*

Adapted from *Helping Women Recover*. Copyright 1999, revised 2008 and 2019 by S. Covington. This material is used by permission of John Wiley & Sons, Inc.

Gratitude

Write down one thing you've gained from working on Step Eleven that you're grateful for.

EXAMPLES:

I am more aware of myself being in tune with my Higher Power.

I finally have a way of praying that feels right for me.

STEP TWELVE

Having had a spiritual awakening as the result of these steps, we tried to carry this message to alcoholics, and to practice these principles in all our affairs.

Step Twelve is not the end of the recovery process. We have stepped onto a path that leads to a new way of life—the best part of our lives is just beginning. In this ongoing journey, we think of *spiritual awakening, practicing the principles,* and *carrying the message.*

Our spiritual awakening is our new connection to something deeper and greater than our own resources. Our new awareness of a Higher or an Inner Power makes us whole. It can be dramatic or gradual; it can involve accepting ourselves and the past, changing our interpretations of past events, finding a peaceful center inside, cultivating hope, and even feeling new sensations in our bodies.

Working all Twelve Steps teaches us to *talk the talk* of recovery. We learn slogans like *First things first, One day at a time,* and *Turn it over.* Practicing the principles means making a habit of *walking the walk*—consistently living each day according to these slogans and other principles. With practice, it becomes more and more natural for us to accept the things we cannot change, change the things we can, ask for help, and turn inward for a quiet place.

Carrying the message to others doesn't require us to become salespeople or representatives of a program. Instead, it's our chance to give genuinely from ourselves, to give our real experience, strength, and hope. Sharing our stories helps us appreciate how alive and aware we've become. Paradoxically, we keep our recovery by giving it away. This is an experience of mutuality, of constant giving and receiving.

In this final chapter you'll think about how the principles of recovery can apply to other areas of your life, and you'll reflect on how you can carry the message to others.

Spiritual Awakening

1. Imagine you're telling a friend or your sponsor about your experience of spiritual awakening. What would you say?

> I believe I have had a spiritual awakening as a result of these Steps. And spiritual awakening is a continual awakening. It's like I am continually coming back to myself. I feel like I've almost come full circle in a way, and that where I'm starting now is where I left off some time ago. Now spirituality is something inside of me. I feel more appreciative of the connection we all have with everything. For me, spirituality is a coming back, a reconnecting.
>
> — MARY LYNN —

Practicing the Principles

2. Below are a few of the principles you've learned in recovery. For each one, describe how you've used it in your recovery and how you can use the principle in another part of your life.

Principle	How I've used this principle in recovery	How I can use this principle elsewhere in my life
Turning it over		
Taking my own inventory		
Creating healthy connections with others		

> Until I began to recover, I never allowed myself to be around the kind of people I respected—people who were creative and successful in their inner as well as outer lives. I had an "addiction" to deprivation, and I wouldn't allow myself to have gratifying relationships. Gradually, I've become able to accept more and more gratification, and the quality of my relationships has increased. The people I allow myself to hang out with are fun to be with, offer me love and support, and encourage and stimulate my creative efforts.
>
> — JACKIE —

Carrying the Message

3. Here are a few of the ways in which you might carry the message to others:

    - speaking in meetings
    - being a sponsor
    - telling your story to people who ask
    - inviting someone with addiction to a meeting
    - living by the principles of recovery
    - volunteering in a hospital, jail, or other institution
    - being of service: setting up, running, or helping with meetings

    Up until now, how have you carried the message to others?

How would you like to carry the message to others during the next six months or so? (Remember that you can give away only what you actually have and that there's no pressure on you to perform.)

> What I learned in the program was that I was connected to other people and . . . there was no "alone." There was nowhere else to go—I wasn't going to go off the planet—I was not without a connection. Being able to be present with and feel the otherness opened my larger sense of relatedness with a Higher Power. The Steps opened me up to that new level of relationship.
>
> — GRACE —

Self-Soothing: Serenity Prayer

Congratulations! By this point in your recovery, you are probably aware of your life spiraling upward and outward into ever-widening circles of self-knowledge, freedom, and connection with others. In the beginning, you applied the principles of recovery just to your addiction, but now—as your life is no longer constricted around the object of your addiction—you can apply the principles throughout your life.

As a final self-soothing skill, consider how the Serenity Prayer could apply to some area of your life other than your addiction. Here's the prayer:

> God, grant me the serenity
>
> to accept the things I cannot change,
>
> courage to change the things I can,
>
> and wisdom to know the difference.

In what area of your life do you currently need this serenity, courage, and wisdom? Say the Serenity Prayer. (Consider memorizing it for use in moments of stress.) Open yourself to help from your Inner or Higher Power. What can you change, and what can't you change?

When you reflect on the work you have been doing for your recovery and think of it as a flower, how would you describe what is blossoming in you now?

Gratitude

Write down one thing you've gained from working on Step Twelve that you're grateful for.

EXAMPLES:

The principles of recovery are more and more a part of my habits.

I feel I've offered something valuable to someone else.

APPENDIX

Twelve Step Prayers

The Third Step Prayer

God, I offer myself to Thee—to build with me and to do with me as Thou wilt. Relieve me of the bondage of self, that I may better do Thy will. Take away my difficulties, that victory over them may bear witness to those I would help of Thy Power, Thy Love, and Thy Way of life. May I do Thy will always![1]

The Seventh Step Prayer

My Creator, I am now willing that you should have all of me, good and bad. I pray that you now remove from me every single defect of character which stands in the way of my usefulness to you and my fellows. Grant me strength, as I go out from here, to do your bidding.[2]

The Eleventh Step Prayer

Lord, make me a channel of thy peace—that where there is hatred, I may bring love—that where there is wrong, I may bring the spirit of forgiveness—that where there is discord, I may bring harmony—that where there is error, I may bring truth—that where there is doubt, I may bring faith—that where there is despair, I may bring hope—that where there are shadows, I may bring light—that where there is sadness, I may bring joy. Lord, grant that I may seek rather to comfort than to be comforted—to understand than to be understood—to love, than to be loved. For it is by self-forgetting that one finds. It is by forgiving that one is forgiven. It is by dying that one awakens to Eternal Life.[3]

The Serenity Prayer

God, grant me the serenity

to accept the things I cannot change,

courage to change the things I can,

and wisdom to know the difference.

NOTES

Step Five

1. "We will not regret the past nor wish to shut the door on it" is from *Alcoholics Anonymous,* 4th ed. (New York: Alcoholics Anonymous World Services, 2001), 83.

Step Six

1. "We claim spiritual progress rather than spiritual perfection" is from *Alcoholics Anonymous,* 4th ed. (New York: Alcoholics Anonymous World Services, 2001), 60.

Step Eleven

1. Stephanie Covington, *A Woman's Way through the Twelve Steps,* 30th anniversary ed. (Center City, MN: Hazelden, 2023), 186.

Appendix

1. Alcoholics Anonymous, *Alcoholics Anonymous,* 4th ed. (New York: Alcoholics Anonymous World Services, 2001), 63.

2. *Alcoholics Anonymous,* 76.

3. Alcoholics Anonymous, *Twelve Steps and Twelve Traditions* (New York: Alcoholics Anonymous World Services, 1981), 99.

ABOUT THE AUTHOR

Stephanie S. Covington, PhD, LCSW, is an internationally recognized clinician, organizational consultant, lecturer, author, and pioneer in the fields of addiction and trauma. For more than thirty-five years, she has created gender-responsive and trauma-informed programs and curricula for use in public, private, and criminal-legal settings, across the US and globally.

Dr. Covington's experience with addiction began with her own life: she became a social drinker who woke up numerous times over the years to no recollection of the night before. On one of those mornings, she woke up afraid, confused, and finally able to acknowledge to herself that she needed help. Thus began day one of a transformative recovery journey, forty-five years and counting, that fixed her on a goal of helping other women reclaim their lives as she had.

Her extensive experience includes consulting for and developing programs for numerous US and international agencies and designing women's services at the Betty Ford Center. She has published extensively, including twelve gender-responsive, trauma-informed treatment curricula and the first manualized treatment program for substance use disorder. Educated at Columbia University and the Union Institute, Dr. Covington is the codirector of both the Institute for Relational Development and the Center for Gender & Justice, which are located in Del Mar, California.

www.stephaniecovington.com

www.centerforgenderandjustice.org

ALSO BY THE AUTHOR

Awakening Your Sexuality: A Guide for Recovering Women

Becoming Trauma Informed: A Training for Staff Development

Beyond Anger and Violence: A Program for Women

Beyond Trauma: A Healing Journey for Women

Beyond Violence: A Prevention Program for Criminal Justice–Involved Women

Exploring Trauma+: A Brief Intervention for Men and Gender-Diverse People with Shane S. Pugh and Roberto R. Rodriguez

Healing Trauma+: A Brief Intervention for Women and Gender-Diverse People with Eileen M. Russo

Helping Men Recover: A Program for Treating Addiction with Dan Griffin and Rick Dauer

Helping Men Recover: A Program for Treating Addiction (criminal justice edition) with Dan Griffin and Rick Dauer

Helping Women Recover: A Program for Treating Addiction

Helping Women Recover: A Program for Treating Addiction (criminal justice edition)

Hidden Healers: The Unexpected Ways Women in Prison Help Each Other Survive

Leaving the Enchanted Forest: The Path from Relationship Addiction to Intimacy with Liana Beckett

Moving from Trauma-Informed to Trauma-Responsive: A Training Program for Organizational Change with Sandra L. Bloom

Voices: A Program of Self-Discovery and Empowerment for Girls with Kimberley Covington and Madeline Covington

A Woman's Way through the Twelve Steps book

A Woman's Way through the Twelve Steps Facilitator Guide

Women and Addiction: A Gender-Responsive Approach

Women in Recovery: Understanding Addiction

A Young Man's Guide to Self-Mastery with Roberto A. Rodriguez

Note: Following the chapters exploring the Steps in *A Woman's Way through the Twelve Steps* are chapters on the topics of self, relationships, sexuality, and spirituality. If you're interested in exploring these areas of life more deeply, see *A Woman's Journal*, the workbook that corresponds with the *Helping Women Recover* program.

PUBLICACIONES EN ESPAÑOL

Ayudar a las mujeres en recuperación: Un programa para tratar las adicciones, Diario de una mujer (*Helping Women Recover: A Program for Treating Addiction, A Woman's Journal*)

Ayudar a las mujeres en recuperación: Un programa para tratar las adicciones, Diario de una mujer, Edición especial para uso en el sistema de justicia (*Helping Women Recover: A Program for Treating Addiction, A Woman's Journal,* special edition for use in the criminal justice system)

Ayudar a los hombres en su recuperación: Un programa para tratar las adicciones, Cuaderno de trabajo (*Helping Men Recover: A Program for Treating Addiction* workbook)

Ayudar a los hombres en su recuperación: Un programa para tratar las adicciones, Cuaderno de trabajo, Edición especial para uso en el sistema de justicia (*Helping Men Recover: A Program for Treating Addiction* workbook, special edition for use in the justice system)

Construyendo una capacidad de recuperación: Libro de ejercicios para hombres y personas con diversidad de género (*Building Resilience: A Workbook for Men and Gender-Diverse People,* part of the *Exploring Trauma+* curriculum, on flash drive)

Más allá de la violencia: Un programa de prevención para mujeres en el sistema penitenciario, Libro de trabajo (*Beyond Violence: A Prevention Program for Criminal Justice–Involved Women* workbook)

La mujer y su práctica de los Doce Pasos (*A Woman's Way through the Twelve Steps*)

La mujer y su práctica de los Doce Pasos, Libro de ejercicios (*A Woman's Way through the Twelve Steps Workbook*)

Mujeres en recuperación: Entendiendo la adicción (*Women in Recovery: Understanding Addiction*)

La sanación del trauma: Libro de ejercicios para mujeres y personas con diversidad de género (*Healing Trauma+: A Workbook for Women and Gender-Diverse People,* part of the *Healing Trauma+* curriculum, on flash drive)

Voces: Un programa de autodescubrimiento y empoderamiento para chicas, Diario (*Voices: A Program of Self-Discovery and Empowerment for Girls* journal)